The Sun Shone

by Maggie Wolcott
(Margaret Alice Wolcott)

**Caton, New York
Steuben County**

January 1, 1879 - March 7, 1880

transcribed by Diane Janowski

New York History Review Press
Elmira, New York

The Sun Shone

by "Maggie" Margaret Alice Wolcott
Transcribed by Diane Janowski
Copyright © 2022 New York History Review Press

Published by New York History Review Press
Elmira, New York

Notice of Rights. All rights reserved. No part of this book may be reproduced or transmitted in any form by any means, electronic, mechanical, photocopying, recording or otherwise, without the prior written permission of the author. For more information on getting permission for reprints and excerpts, contact us through our website.
www.NewYorkHistoryReview.com

ISBN: 978-0-9994192-9-8
First Edition

Printed in the United States of America

Maggie's diary in its current condition.
Courtesy of the Eleanor Barnes Library, Elmira, NY

Table of Contents

Foreward..8
Maps of Caton..10, 11
People in the Diary..12
The Sun Shone...15
Wolcott Pedigree..66
Afterward..67
Bibiliography..68

Foreward

In our *Learning from History* series of Upstate New York diaries, accounts of young people's lives on the farm, or in the home, help us to understand their thoughts and experiences. Each narrative offers a unique perspective on young peoples' lives in rural New York, and serves as an important primary resource in the study of American history.

The Sun Shone is the journal of 14-year-old "Maggie" Margaret Alice Wolcott of Caton, New York - six miles south of Corning, New York.

Maggie was born on August 13, 1864 in Steuben County, the youngest of four children of Archibald and Cornelia Wolcott. She had three older sisters - Aurealia, called "Real," Frances called "Frank," and Ella. All lived nearby with their husbands.

Beginning on January 1, 1879, Maggie recorded the events of her life in a small 2½ x 3¾ inch pocket diary with three entries to the page in very nice handwriting. Maggie's notations were confined to the spaces allotted and are written in pencil. Her handwriting is mostly legible, except for a few names or places that cannot be deciphered. Maggie's spelling is left as she spelled it. Clarifications have been added in brackets. The photographed pages from her diary are actual size.

Young Maggie lived with her parents. She had plenty of friends and neighbors. She was generally very happy in her life – she enjoyed her family, friends, church, and household chores. Her father had a farm at today's 2466 Ginnan Road in Caton, New York. She especially liked going to the nearby city of Corning to do errands. Maggie did much work in her home and also helped her sisters and neighbors.

The Sun Shone invites us into the daily life of a New York young woman through her own words and experiences. We hear Maggie's voice as she shares his joys, sorrows, enthusiasm, and fragility of life in a rural farming community.

The Eleanor Barnes Library acquired Maggie Wolcott's diary in 2010. So far as is known, this transcription is its first published version. The photographs of Caton are by Allen C. Smith.

Diane Janowski, Publisher

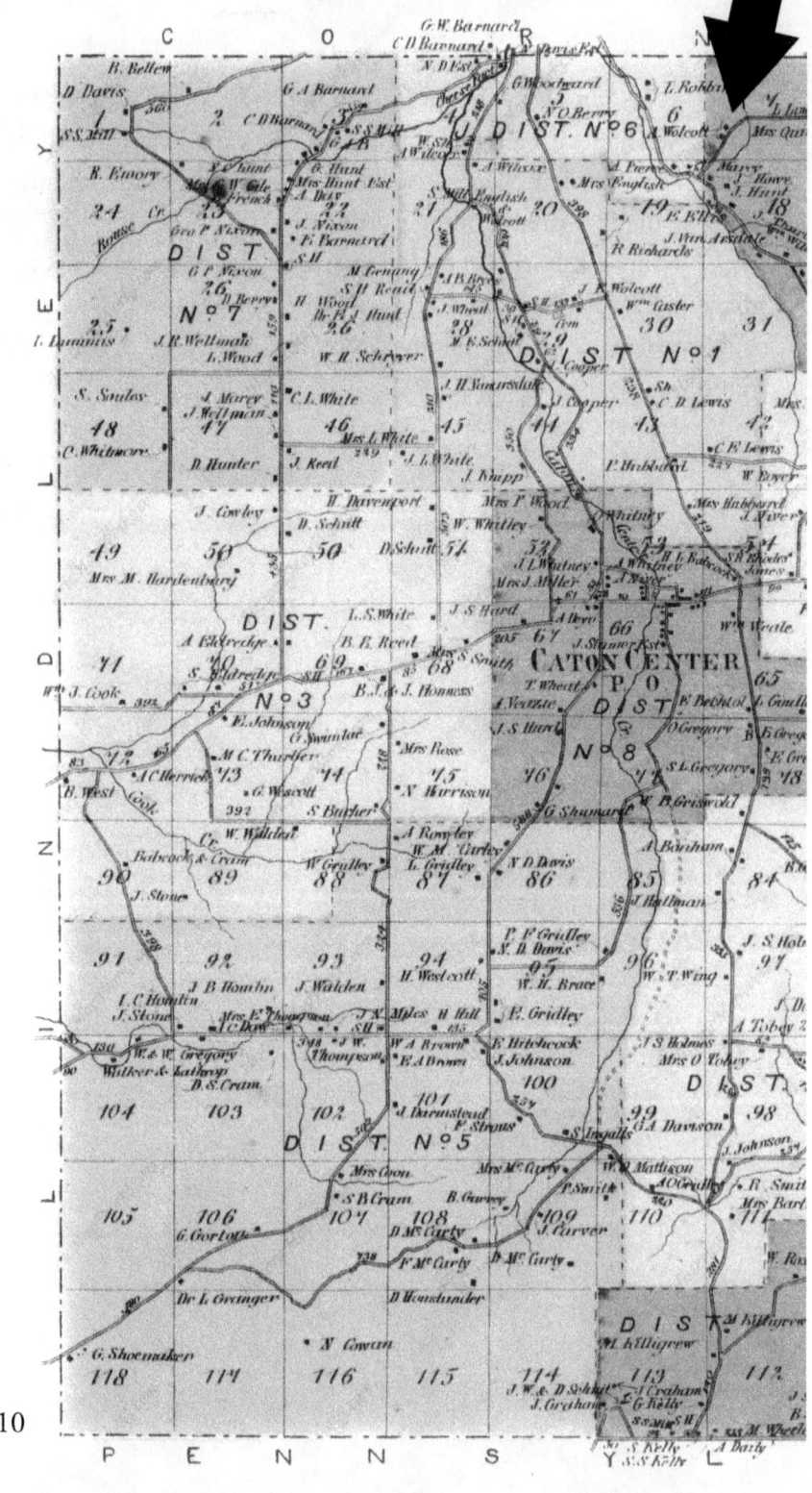

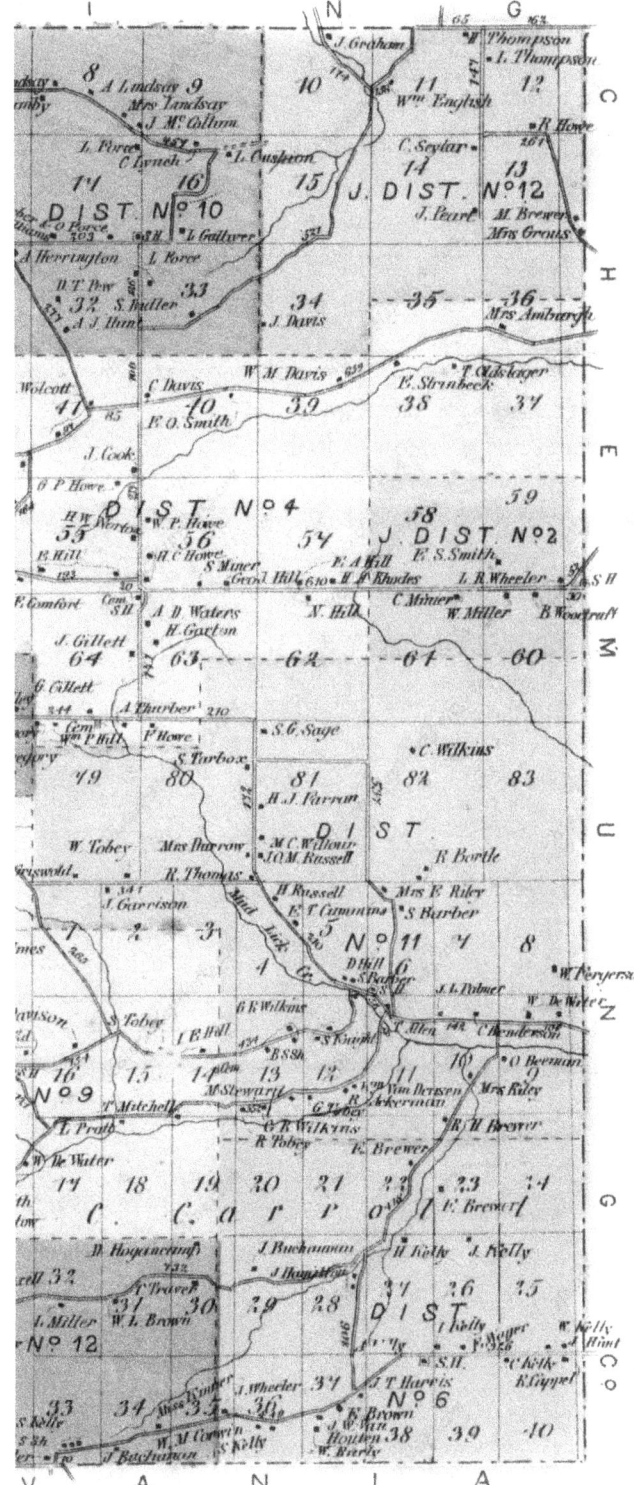

Map of Caton, New York area, 1873. The arrow on the opposite page indicates the Wolcott home.

People in the diary
Maggie's family

Pa - Archibald Smith Wolcott - age 49, farmer in Caton
Ma - Cornelia Hunt - age 44
Grampa – Joseph Hunt age 86, lived nearby
Aurelia "Real" Seyter - age 24, older sister, lived next door, married to Albert Albert "Birt" Seyter - brother-in-law, farmhand, married to Aurelia
Frances "Frank" Force – age 26, older sister – milliner married to Oscar   Oscar Force - age 30, farmer, brother-in-law
Ella French- age 21, older sister married to Albert [Tid], lived in Corning
Albert "Tid" French - age 23, brother-in-law, farmer, married to Ella

Friends and Relations

Julian Babcock - age 34, farmer in Caton
Irena Barnard – age 11, lived in Corning
Becktel
Thelma Bundy
Cora
Miss Cowen teacher
Aunt Delilah
Flora
Frank and Hattie Force
Miss French
Gershom "Girsh" Bernard – age 44, surveyor, lived in Corning
Flora [Bundy?]
Mr. Gorton
Gosger
Herrington's
Ettie Howe – age 13, lived in Caton

Howe
Irene [Hunt?] age 10
Aunt Jane Hunt
Jane
Rachel Labar
Mr. Job Marcy – age 58, farmer, lived next door
Therista "Ist" Marcy – age 20, lived next door
Dr. Henry C. May – doctor in Corning, age 48
Dr. T. Augustus Mills – doctor in Corning at 257 Locust Street
Nealy Nivers
Osley
Mrs Richards - lived nearby
Anna Robinson
Marion Robin
Lucy Seiber
Charlie Snider
Aurelia Straubinger
Mary Straubinger
Tom Straubringer - age 54, mason, from Germany, lived in Corning
Addie Teeter
Lizzie Teeter
Alice Thurber - age 30, lived in Caton
John V (shot himself)
"Mattie" Matthias Welles - age 60, lumberman from Elmira, NY
Hattie Wilcok
George Wolcott
Tim Wolcott - age 7, younger cousin
Mr. Wesket
Bill Williams (Died Aug 21)
Woodard (baby died Jan 27 1879)

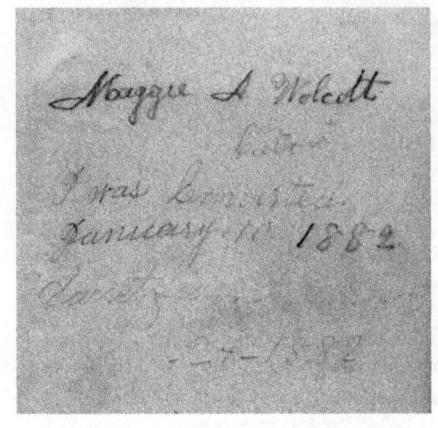

I was Converted January 10, 1882
Sanctified January 24, 1882

Maggie A. Wolcott
Caton, New York

January, Wednesday 1, 1879
I went down to Ella's. Real [Aurelia] went down to Mate's—and to Ella's. I want to got to Tim's. Pa went to Grampa's to kill squirrels.   Rote in Flora's album.

January, Thursday 2, 1879
I went to school. Tid and I played cards. Mr. Wesket died and is going to be buried tomorrow. It snows.

January, Friday 3, 1879
I went to Cirrels. It was cold. I could not go home. I went to school and there wasn't but six scholars.

January, Saturday 4, 1879
I went home and I was cold. Ella had the headache. I washed my stockins and getted some chickens. At night played cards.

January, Sunday 5, 1879
Frank [her sister Frances] and Oscar came down today and the children. I have a sore throte – a canker or something else. It is modret [moderate] today and snowed a little.

January, Monday 6, 1879
It snowed today. Ella and Tid come up tonight. My throte is worse tonight. Pa went to mill. Kild too cats. We washed today.

January, Tuesday 7, 1879
My cold is better. I stayed to home yesterday and today. Birt went to Corning with a load of hay. The sun shone. It has been snowing since Christmas.

January, Wednesday 8, 1879
I went to school today. It is a nice day. Pa brought me down to Ella's this morning. Pieced blocks tonight. Tid caught 3 mice.

January, Thursday 9, 1879
Irena came down. Stayed all night with us. We made her into a cabbage, chicken ---- in Tid's clothes. It snowed today.

January, Friday 10, 1879
I received a present from Addie Teeter today. I come home today. Aunt Hanna's family was over to our house today. Grampa got a present from the West.

January, Saturday 11, 1879
✝ Pa and Birt went to Corning. I mopped. Birt got a dog in Corning. It snowed part of the day. Pa went to Grampa's and Jane got a present. [Maggie made the sign of the cross every month]

January, Sunday 12, 1879
The sun shone all day. In the evening Kitt and Ella & Tid come up. I come home with them. I drove my headache. Mr. Gorton come down.

January, Monday 13, 1879
Nice day. I stade to Ella's. Ella went home. Flora stade with me. I went to school. A peddler come to Ella's. I dressed up in man's clothes just for fun.

January, Tuesday 14, 1879
I went to school. It snowed a little too. Lizzie Teeter was married the 8th of January. I peaced blocks.

January, Wednesday 15, 1879
I come home tonight. Rachel Labar and Charlie Snider. I went to school. It snowed this evening. Birt come after me.

January, Friday 10. 1879.

I received a present from Addie tacher to me I come home to day aunt hanna farley was to our house to day granpaw got a present bureau like mine

Saturday 11.

pa and Bill went off sawing I moped Bill got a day to coming it showed full of all day pa was gaun pas and John got a present

Sunday 12.

the sun shone all day in the evening Lott and Ella Cat came up i come home with them i drove my head ach has gotten come down

January, Monday 13. 1879.

nice day i stade to Ellas Ella went home
Pilosa stade with me I went to school a fodder come to Ellas i dressed up in mens clothes prof for fun

Tuesday 14.

I went to school it snow-ed a little to. Lizzie Laty was married the 8 of January i peaced lass

Wednesday 15.

I come home to night rachell Lobar and I ride I guder I went to schol it snowed this evening Bill come after me

January, Thursday 16, 1879
I went to Frank's and the company. We all went to Ella's in the evening. It snowed in the morning. The sun shone in the afternoon. I had the headache and Real, Birt and Rachel.

January, Friday 17, 1879
The sun shone, The company went away. Pa and Birt went to Corning. I peaced [pieced] medley. It is cloudy this evening. I stade to home today and yesterday.

January, Saturday 18, 1879
The sun shone. Birt and Aurelia went to George Wolcott. I washed and ironed. My head ached. I cut out medleys for Irena [Barnard].

January, Sunday 19, 1879
The sun shone. Charley Seyter's family was to our house. My throat is sore. Another --- in my throat.

January, Monday 20, 1879
Pleasant in the morning. Snowed about 9 oclock. I rode down with Orly to Ella's family. I went to school.

January, Tuesday 21, 1879
Nice day. It snowed in the afternoon. I went to school. Had a nice time. Played cards in the evening with Tid. He beat me.

January, Wednesday 22, 1879
The sun shone all day. I went to school. Minnie Barnard and Sam come down this evening. We all went to Elmira. Got me a dress.

January, Thursday 23, 1879
Sun shone. I went to Irena Barnard's. I had a nice time. Cora brought me a Medley [a quilt piece]. Minnie gave me some calico and her mother.

January, Friday 24, 1879
The sun shone. I come home from Ella's with Pa and Ma. Real got some calico for Medley. Dunbar come up to fix the melodian.

January, Saturday 25, 1879
The sun shone part of the day. George Wolcott's folks came up to our house. Ella come up with them. My throat is soar.

January, Sunday 26, 1879
The sun shone. Tid and Ella and Kit come up to our house and our band. My throat is soar. I went home with them. I drove.

January, Monday 27, 1879
It raned. I went to school. My throat is soar. Miss Cowen is to Miss French's and her girl. Mr. Woodard's little baby dide. Fred and Eddie set up.

January, Tuesday 28, 1879
The sun shone. I dident go to school. I went to Corning to see Dr. Mills – went with Birt. Ella went to the furnel [funeral]. I got me a thimble.

January, Wednesday 29, 1879
Nice day I went to school. I went up to Irena and Ella and Tid. I had a nice time. Miss Cowen was there.

January, Thursday 30, 1879
Nice day. I went to school I stade to Ella's. The stove man come. Pa shelled corn.

January, Friday 31, 1879
The sun shone. I went to school. I rode down hill. I come home a-foot. Pa shelled corn.

February, Saturday 1, 1879
I stade to home. Ella and Tid come home. I pealed sweet apples. Kit come home tonight.

February, Sunday 2, 1879
I come down to Ella's. Lib was there in a eater? Ella and Tid went to Girsh's [Gershom Bernard] to hear the band play.

February, Monday 3. 1879.

the sun shone part of the day and it sno[w]ed I went to school miss cowen come to lift[?] from us Barnard my head ached Marion Robert and Lowe

Tuesday 4.

it snowed all day i went to school I went to Emma's Bar nards I and Elora and stade all night had a nice time rode down hill and played concersion

Wednesday 5.

snowed I went to school Emma Effa[?] came slep with me Luna come over from schol and pa up with Ted Ella went up to Emmas & Ed went after tea

February, Thursday 6. 1879.

cloudy I went to schol I had the head ache miss Cowen went up to Jessies Barnard pa went to mrs harrington

Friday 7.

sun shone i went to school I went home Birt drawed logs and I rode up with him a log rolled on pas leg this afternoon we went home to Ellas this evening

Saturday 8.

sun shone pa ses I coul go to school eny more we washed and iorned Birt went to leaning[?] an got some bark

February, Monday 3, 1879
The sun shone part of the day and it snowed. I went to school. Miss Cowen came to Ella's from us Barnard. My head ached. Marion Robin cane down.

February, Tuesday 4, 1879
It snowed a little. I went to school. I went to Emma Barnard's. I and Flora and stade all night. Had a nice time. Rode downhill and played dominoes.

February, Wednesday 5, 1879
Snowed. I went to school from Emma's. Ella Cowen slept with me. Irena come over from school and rode up with Tid. Ella went up to Emma's, Tid went after her.

February, Thursday 6, 1879
Cloudy. I went to school. I had the headache. Miss Cowen went up to Girsh Barnard's. Pa went to Mrs. Harrington.

February, Friday 7, 1879
Sun shone. I went to school. I went home. Birt drawed logs and I rode up with him. A log rolled on Pa's leg this afternoon. We went down to Ella's this morning.

February, Saturday 8, 1879
Sun shone. Pa says I can't go to school anymore. We washed and mopped. Birt went to Corning and got some fish.

February, Sunday 9, 1879
Sun shone. Pa went to Grampa's and killed a muskrat. I had the headache. Ma had the stomachache.

February, Monday 10, 1879
Sun shone. Real and I ironed. Pa moved up stairs. Carried the stove up alone. Ma was sick this morning. Pa went to Corning and got a new lamb.

February, Tuesday 11, 1879
Rained. Pa went to town meeting and Birt slicked up the back room.

February, Wednesday 12, 1879
Sun shone part of the day. Ma and Pa went to Ella's. I peaced Medley.

February, Thursday 13, 1879
Sun shone. Birt went a-hunting. I peaced blocks. I commenced a nightdress. I got a scolding.

February, Friday 14, 1879
Nice day. Birt went to Corning. Finished nightdress. Commenced some blankets. I helped about the moving.

February, Saturday 15, 1879
Nice day. I finished the blankets. Pa went to Corning – got the horses shod – got some medicine. Oscar was hear and Ed Cole got the hams.

February, Saturday 16, 1879
Nice day. In the evening Ella and Miss French and Tid and Miss Cowen come up. I read in the Bible. Gorge preached at night.

February, Sunday 17, 1879
Snowed in the afternoon. John Smith's hound come. Birt chained him up. We washed. Started milking. Masons come.

February, Tuesday 18, 1879
It snowed. I peaced in the evening. I sewed up my black dress skirt. Pa set up with Mr. Harrington.

February, Wednesday 19, 1879
Nice day. Ella French come. Pa and Birt went to Corning. Had a fuss. I ironed some.

February, Thursday 20, 1879
Birt set up with Mr. Harrington. Squally today. I went to Ella's about 5 minutes and to Mr. Harrington's. Pa and I. Tom was up. Forces went to see Uncle Gos.

February, Friday 21, 1879
Nice day. Miss Bechtel dide tonight. Went to the dance with Osley's Folks. I went. - had a nice time. Ettie and Emma come with Kitt. I danced 5 sets.

February, Saturday 22, 1879
Nice day. I got up at half-past 11 o'clock. Pa went to Corning to see the doctor. May Olson is sick with the long fever.

February, Sunday 23, 1879
Bad day. I stade to home. Ella and Tid come in the evening. They had been to Voser's – Fred and his wife was there. Frank has got a bad cold.

February, Monday 24, 1879
Nice day. Ma is sick. Mr. Harrington is worse. Pa is better. Birt drawed wood. We washed. Coal stove broke.

February, Tuesday 25, 1879
Snowed all day. Ma is sick. Birt went and set up with Mr. Harrington. I peaced medley.

February, Wednesday 26, 1879
Birt went to Corning. Wednesday. Nice day. I ironed. Ella was up in the evening and Tid and Birt went up to Frank & Oscar. Wanted [to] sell Birt his dog Mickie.

February, Thursday 27, 1879
Nice day. Tide [tied] Real's quilt. Tide some in the evening.

February, Friday 28, 1879
Nice day. I went to Mr. Marcy and Ettie Howe come there. I had the toothache.

March, Saturday 1, 1879
Nice day. I moped. Birt drawed wood.

March, Sunday 2, 1879
Nice day. Ella and Tid come in the evening. Pa's heifer had a calf. She was sick. Tid and Birt went after Mr. Niver. I went to Grampa's.

March, Monday 3, 1879
Nice day. We washed. Sewed carpet rags in the evening.

March, Tuesday 4, 1879
Nice day. I went to Corning to see [Dr.] May. He gave me some medicine. Oscar [Force] stopped in the morning. Simon went with him. Birt and Real and Pa went to Oscar's – got a hog.

March, Wednesday 5, 1879
Nice day. I went to Mr. Marcy in the afternoon. Birt and Real and I went to Ella's in the evening. Pa went to Mr. Marcy at night. We stade alone.

March, Thursday 6, 1879
Snowed in the morning. Pa and Birt drawed logs. Ma is making her dress. Sewed carpet rags in the evening. My head ached part of the day.

March, Friday 7, 1879
Nice day. I went to Corning to Anna Broson. I went to Dr. May's. She rode up with us. She stopped to Mr. Howe – staid all night with Ettie. Frank and Oscar was down.

March, Saturday 8, 1879
We had a thundershower at night. Frank and Real and Ella and Maggie went to Corning. We had our pictures taken. I went to Mr. Howe's.

March, Sunday 9, 1879
Nice day. I and Anna and Ettie and Thristy and Clem went up to Flora Bundy's. Anna stade all night with me and Clem. Ettie come up for the first time since they was mad.

March, Monday 10, 1879
Nice day. Anna and I and Clem and Pa and Ma went to funeral. Went around by French's. Anna stayed all night with me. Aurelia set up with Aunt Jane Hunt.

March, Tuesday 11, 1879
Rained this evening. Nice day. Anna went to Ettie. Clem went home. Pa and I went to Corning – Dr. May's. Went to Grampa's. Pa went there this evening.

March, Wednesday 12, 1879
Nice day. I ironed. Frank and Oscar and the children come down in the evening. The thunderstorm Saturday night struck a man and 2 horses and a cow and Mr. Strubeck's house.

March, Thursday 13, 1879
Nice day. The wind blew. I went to Grampa's. Aunt Jane is worse. Birt and Real went up to Oscar's tonight. Mr. Marcy come up after Pa to go to Grampa's.

March, Friday 14, 1879
Snowed a little in the morning. I went to Grampa's twice and to Mr. Marcy after some slippery elm. Ma got the headache. Real feels bad. My head aches. Frances sent her peaces.

March, Saturday 15, 1879
Nice day. The wind blew. I mopped. Birt went to Corning. Oscar come and got Real's calf. Pa went to Grampa's. Birt found his dog. Tid sold his horse.

March, Sunday 16, 1879
Nice day. I went to Grampa's and stayed [til] 5 o'clock. Ella and Tid come up. 6 folks come to Grampa's. Ella, Ettie and Jacob, Miss Robins. Aunt Jane is better. Ma is sick.

March, Monday 17, 1879
Nice day, Frank and Archie and Lee, and Oscar come down. Birt and Oscer went to Corning. Got our pictures that was for Ma and Pa. Set up with Aunt Jane.

March, Tuesday 18, 1879
We washed. Nice day. Frank and Birt and Ella went to Corning. Took the pictures back. Oscar and Edd Cole come down and brought the calf.

March, Wednesday 19, 1879
Nice day. I went to Grampa's. Stayed all day. Ettie come up there. Aunt Nancy [Toby] and Clarcy come to Grampa's. Real cut out my dress and her's.

March, Thursday 20, 1879
Nice day. I went to Corning and Real and Ella and Frank went to get out profiles.

March, Friday, 21, 1879
Nice day. We sewed on my wrapper. Pa took a load of hay to Dr. May. Tid and Birt went a-hunting.

March, Saturday 22, 1879
Stormy. I went to Grampa's in the morning and got breakfast for him. I mopped. My head ached. Ella and Tid come up and stade all night.

March, Sunday 23, 1879
Cloudy today. Tid and Ella stayed all day. Frank and Oscar and the children come down this evening.

March, Monday 24, 1879
Nice day. We washed. Pa went after cows. Went to John Wolcott. Birt and Tid went a-hunting.

March, Tuesday 25, 1879
Nice day. I ironed in the forenoon. Went up to Callie and Carrie this afternoon. Emma Barnard come up to Ettie. I stopped to Marcy's.

March, Wednesday 26, 1879
Cloudy. We got a little lamb – it is lame. Worked on my apron. Ma commenced her Irish chain [kind of a quilt].

March, Thursday 27, 1879
Cloudy. I finished my apron. Pieced on Ma's chain. Tom and Tim come up. Mixed the bread.

March, Friday 28, 1879
Cloudy. Pa and Birt went to Corning and got our pictures. The dog John run off. Clem come and stayed all night. Den [Dennis] Barnard's house burned yestardy.

March, Saturday 29, 1879
Rained. Clem went home. Pa and Birt went after cows – got 2. Pa saw Tim. I mopped. Betty has got a lamb. We worked on Ma's chain.

March, Sunday 30, 1879
Cloudy. I finished reading *The Boy Emigrants*. I have got to *Romans* in the Bible. We got another lamb. We was alone all day.

March, Monday 31, 1879
Nice day. Ma washed. Oscar come down – got the profiles. Pa killed the calf and took it to Corning.

April, Tuesday 1, 1879
We had a lamb. Sun shone. I ironed. Ma went up to Aunt Delia's. Birt went up to Oscar's and got the dog machine. Real and Flora come down.

April, Wednesday 2, 1879
Snowed a little. Wind blew west. Ma commenced joining her chain. The hog had pigs. I was going to Ella's but it is cold.

April, Thursday 3, 1879
Cloudy – 2 years ago today Ella and Birt and I went to Corning and got her tooth out. The men drawed wood.

April, Friday 4, 1879
Julian Babcock died today. 2 years ago today Aurelia and Albert was married. We are joining my 4 squares. Another lamb. Pa and Birt drawed wood. We had a custard.

April, Friday 4. *Side 1879.* *Julian Babcock*
to day owed 2 years ago to day Aurelia and Albert was married We are going my Squay Another lamp pa and Birt drawed wood we had a custard

Saturday 5.
snowed I stoped I went to Ellas Kit was up to Julias Sunday pa went to morning Shad and night Ella has a New Stove

Sunday 6.
Nice day I stade to Ellas till 3 oclock Jid and Ella brought me home Julian Babcock was buried Betty is sick aida Christion dide a while ago

April, Plesont **Monday 7.** 1879.
We washed Aurelia was sick Mrs Elice & Bettys better Edd cole come down Birt went to corning pa went to alan linsy Vendue

Tuesday 8.
Nice day aint delila come I Irned Biond Jy come her aunt Delilah I Begun to Smoke Cubebs the men Sawed wood Frank and archey come down a foot

Wednesday 9.
Nice Day I went up to Boyer and got the Doy till patzin Ma put on her vist Chang the men sawed wood

April, Saturday 5, 1879
Snowed. I mopped. I was to Ella. Kit was up to Julia Bundy's. Pa went to Corning. Stayed all night. Ella has a new stove.

April, Sunday 6, 1879
Nice day. I stayed to Ella's till 3 o'clock. Tid and Ella brought me home. Julian Babcock was buried. Betty is sick. Alida Christian died awhile ago.

April, Monday 7, 1879
Pleasant. We washed. Aurelia was sick. Betty is better. Edd Cole come down. Birt went to Corning. Pa went to Alan Linsy's [Allen Linsey's] vendue.

April, Tuesday 8, 1879
Nice day. Aunt Delia. Grampa come here and Delia. I begun to smoke cubes [chubs?]

April, Wednesday 9, 1879
Nice day. I went up to Flora's and got the overall pattern. Ma worked on her Irish chain. The men sawed wood.

April, Thursday 10, 1879
Rained. Mrs. French come up in the Morning. Tid brought her. Mrs. Gorton come down. They quilted. Uncle Jacob come down and brought part of Aunt Delia's dress. The men sawed wood.

April, Friday 11, 1879
Snowed. Good Friday. Ma and I quilted. We roaled 3 times. Birt went to Charlie's and Tom's. One of the horses kicked him. Pa cut wood. Real worked on Birt's overalls.

April, Saturday 12, 1879
Nice day. Birt went to the post to mail. We had twin lambs. I mopped. Ma washed the windows. I pulled a tooth Friday.

April, Sunday 13, 1879
Rained. Tid and Ella come up. Easter Sunday. My head ached.

April, Monday 14, 1879
Pleasant. Ma washed. I ironed. Aurelia boiled hemlock bark. Birt commenced plowing the first time in the afternoon. Pa cut wood. Pa went down to Tid's after the plow.

April, Tuesday 15, 1879
Frank and Emil come down. We quilted. Real colored her wash.

April, Wednesday 16, 1879
Pleasant. I mopped. Kittie and Ella come up a-foot. Real come down to Ella's and Tid come up after them. We quilted. There is a dance up to Mr. Williams' tonight.

April, Thursday 17, 1879
Snowed. I quilted. Real quilted for the first time. Peddler come here Wednesday. Ma got a bacon and some stove polish. Mr. Marcy come up. Birt made a wash bench.

April, Friday 18, 1879
I blacked the stove. We quilted. Birt made two stools. Pa found a mother lamb.

April, Saturday 19, 1879
Pleasant. Ella come up with Papa. Went to Corning after the doctor. Birt went out and got out Hannah. Aurelia is sick. Did come up tonight. A burial tonight.

April, Sunday 20, 1879
Pleasant. We had company – Frank [sister Frances] and her family. Mattie [Matthias] Welles and Uncle Bill and his wife. Tid and Ella.

April, Monday 21, 1879
Pleasant. Ella and I washed. Birt plowed in the forenoon. Pa went to Corning in the afternoon. Delia come down.

April, Tuesday 22, 1879
Pleasant. Ella ironed. I begun to wash in the front yard. Elsie and her children come in the afternoon. Birt plowed today. Ella and I went to Marcy's twice. Real is worse.

April, Wednesday 23, 1879
Cloudy. Rained. Commenced apron. Ripped up Aurelia green dress. Frank and Mollie. Wed come down in the evening. Sowed the peas today. Birt sowed out the first no the orchard.

April, Thursday 24, 1879
Cloudy and sun shone part of the day. Sowed the oats today. Finished my apron & mopped. I washed in the yard. Birt got a crab apple tree.

April, Friday 25, 1879
Pleasant. We made pies and Nancy [Wilkins] come and Uncle Henry [Wilkins]. They are going to start West Tuesday.

April, Saturday 26, 1879
Pleasant in the morning. Rained in the afternoon. It thundered. I went up to Flora's and got a book. Dela Wheat was up to Flora's. We went and gathered flowers. Tid come up. Ma got the first greens for Real. Birt plowed.

April, Sunday 27, 1879
Pleasant. Henry Seyter come up. Tid stayed all night. I finished reading Flora's book. Ella is here now.

April, Monday 28, 1879
Rained. We washed. I made some mitts. All the folks went to sleep but Ma & Pa sorted potatoes. Birt plowed up by the swale [a swampy low tract of land].

April, Tuesday 29, 1879
Pleasant. I went up to Frank's after coal ashes. Fred Brown works there. The leach started to run. Ella commenced to make soap. Birt and Pa went to Corning. Birt took some potatoes. Got one dollar a bushel.

April, Wednesday 30, 1879
Pleasant. I got some greens. Ella finished the soap. We ironed. Birt plowed.

May, Thursday 1, 1879
Cloudy. Ella went home. Birt and I took her. Mrs. Gorton come down in the afternoon. Ella mopped and made bread. Birt plowed. Pa picked stones. We had greens for dinner.

May, Friday 2, 1879
Cloudy. We had onions for dinner. I cut out pieces for Frank and Ma and I. Birt cultivated [the] barley ground. Pa picked stones.

May, Saturday 3, 1879
Pleasant in the morning. Rained at night. We churned, baked pies. Birt sowed barley. Pa dragged it in. I mopped. Real went out in the first room today.

✝ May, Sunday 4, 1879
Cloudy. We was alone. Real came down stairs for the first [time]. Birt and I went up to the field. The oats are staring up. The peas are coming up.

May, Monday 5, 1879
Pleasant. I and Birt started for Ella's. Mate and Charlie come up. Kitt took her carpet rugs to the weaver. Pa and Birt cleared up the wheat. Ella come up with us.

May, Tuesday 6, 1879
Pleasant. Ella washed. I was sick. Pa went to Aunt Hannah Wolcott's funeral. Ella went home - Birt took her. Birt sowed wheat up by the Simon's.

May, Wednesday 7, 1879
Cloudy. I ironed in the afternoon. I went up to Osley's woods and got some dirt. Took up my double scarlet geranium.

May, Thursday 8, 1879
Pleasant. Pa and Birt went to Corning. Birt got Real's crocks and some coffee. Lib [Elisabeth] Barnard broke her leg the other day.

May, Friday 9, 1879
Pleasant. I went to Aunt Delila's. Ettie went to Mrs. Harrington. Ettie come up. Flora and Cora come. I gave Ettie some gladioluses and Delila gave me a little root.

May, Saturday 10, 1879
Pleasant. Ettie and I went to Hattie Wilcox. Hattie gave us some slips. I stopped to Ettie's. Ella got her dishes today.

May, Sunday 11, 1879
Pleasant. Tid and Ella come up. We went up to Oscar's and they was gone. Ella and Tid commenced keeping house. Fanny has got her calf.

May, Monday 12, 1879
Pleasant. Ma washed. Birt and I fed the calf.

May, Tuesday 13, 1879
Pleasant. Birt plowed the gardens and the ditch and got me some sand. I took up some plants. We took the carpet rugs outdoors.

May, Wednesday 14, 1879
Pleasant. We cleaned Real's room. She commenced the scrap rug.

May, Thursday 15, 1879
Pleasant. I cleaned the seller [cellar]. Commenced turning the rugs. It clouded up today. The cherry trees commenced to blossom.

May, Friday 16, 1879
Pleasant. I cleaned the back clospress [clothespress]. Pa and Birt put up the churning machine. John churned the first time. Real is up today. Mrs. French is sick.

May, Saturday 17, 1879
Pleasant. I went to Oscar's. Fred Brown came after me. Mopped. Oscar went up. They got home at 2 o'clock.

MAY, FRIDAY 16. 1879.

Pleasant
I hemmed the back chipues
bar and sent part of the
churning machine
John churned the first time
Joel is 24 to day Mrs
french is sick

SATURDAY 17.

Pleasant
I went to George Souts
Brown came after us
when I got there he was
got home at 10 oclock

SUNDAY 18.

rained a little
Jud and Ellen came up
Ira see us Charlie Allen
came up Frank and I
went to Charlies
they brought me home

MAY, MONDAY 19. 1879.

Pleasant
We washed I went to grand
pas and Ellie and Miss cox
Boal and pa went to court
pa in Allen law suit
But staid down to noon
I got some greens pa got a hat
and some sault

TUESDAY 20.

Pleasant
We cleaned the front room
We churned Boal was
home for dinner

WEDNESDAY 21.

Pleasant
Ellie come up and brought
Ellas book Pleurisy root
and I gave her Ellas
and some seeds We put
down the carpet in the fur
nt room I washed
Ella is 21 to day

May, Sunday 18, 1879
Rained a little. Tid and Ella come up to Oscar's. Charlie Williams come up to Frank and I went to Sharlet's [Charlotte's?]. They brought me home.

May, Monday 19, 1879
Pleasant. We washed. Went to Grandpa's and Ettie and Marcy's. Birt and Pa went to Corning in Allen law suit. Birt stayed down. Real and I got some greens. Pa got a pale and some sault [salt?].

May, Tuesday 20, 1879
Pleasant. We cleaned the front room. We. We churned. Birt come home. Pa plowed.

May, Wednesday 21, 1879
Pleasant. Ettie come up and brought Ella's book. C---- come and I gave her slips and some seeds. We put down the carpet in the front room. Ella is 21 today.

May, Thursday 22, 1879
Pleasant. I ironed. Ma has got the toothache. And I and Real churned. Pa planted cucumber seeds.

May, Friday 23, 1879
Pleasant. I went to Grandpa's this afternoon. Frank is here today. I cleaned out the seller. John churned today. Birt and Pa planted corn today.

May, Saturday 24, 1879
Pleasant. I went out to Jane's this forenoon. Baked. Birt finished planting corn. Aurelia Straubinger come up tonight. Real and Birt went to Sticklertown.

May, Sunday 25, 1879
Pleasant. Mary Straubinger went home. Birt and Real come home. Oscar and Frank come after me to go to Alice Thurber's. Couldn't go. Mary Straubinger has got a baby.

May, Monday 26, 1879
Ma and Real washed. I carried in the planter. Real set out her Lillies of the Valley that Lizzy gave her.

May, Tuesday 27, 1879
Rained. Corn field. We cleaned the dining room and got out the bees wax. Miss Howe gave Grandpa a blowing about the fence that they built up. Birt sowed some plaster and Pa put some strings in the ----.

May, Wednesday 28, 1879
Pleasant. The men picked stone. We cleaned the back room and the front clospress [clothespress]. I took up the carpet in the hall. Frank and the children come down and brought Real's butter.

May, Thursday 29, 1879
Pleasant. Pa went to Corning after plaster. We cleaned the first chamber. Ma ironed. John Vanderwhacker shot himself.

May, Friday 30, 1879
A slight thundershower. Pa and Birt sowed plaster. Tid stopped in front of the house. Shanghi has got a calf. John Vanderwhacker was buried in the afternoon. Pa and Birt sowed plaster.

May, Saturday 31, 1879
Pleasant. Grandpa come and Flora Bundy come this afternoon. Sealia Janson came after. Flora, Orley Gorton, and Mrs. Elice come up with him. The men sowed plaster.

June, Sunday 1, 1879
Rained a little this afternoon. Ma and Pa went to Ella's. Real and I and Birt went up to the field to see an old lady. Pa went up to Grandpa's this evening.

June, Monday 2, 1879
Rained, We cleaned Ma's bedroom. Pa went to the mill. Birt killed a woodchuck.

June, Tuesday 3, 1879
Rained. I went to Grandpa's and to Marcy's after verbenas. We washed.

June, Wednesday 4, 1879
Pleasant. I went to Corning. Ma and I got me a hat and a dress. I set out the verbinas. Real made a tidy.

June, Thursday 5, 1879
Rained. I went to Ella's. Pa walked the sheep. Birt and Pa made a door for the seller [cellar]. We have got some more kittens.

June, Friday 6, 1879
Pleasant. We cleaned the sitting room. I went to Grandpa's. Thristy [Therista or "Ist" Marcy] come up. I caught a blue bird.

June, Saturday 7, 1879
Pleasant. I went to Aunt Delilah's - Ettie and I. It was her birthday. Mary Nixon was here. It was her birthday, she is 14.

June, Sunday 8, 1879
Pleasant. I went to Sunday School with Ettie [probably Ettie Berry]. Tid and Ella brought me home. Ma and Pa went to Oscar's. Alice Thirber [Thurber] was there and Loocy [Lucy] Seiber.

June, Monday 9, 1879
Pleasant. I went to Grandpa's and Marcy's - Ettie and I. Mrs. Gorton came down. Grandpa came over. We worked. We have got apples.

June, Tuesday 10, 1879
Rained in the afternoon. I helped Aunt Jane in the forenoon. I had the headache. We cleaned upstairs. Pa went to see Smith about the cow.

June, Wednesday 11, 1879
Pleasant. I helped Aunt Jane. We cleaned upstairs. I took the Sunday School paper to Ettie Howe.

June, Thursday 12, 1879
Rained in the afternoon. I helped Aunt Jane. I went to Leman Robbins after some tea. Oscar and Frank come down and the children.

June, Friday 13, 1879
Pleasant. I helped Aunt Jane. Birt commenced to plow the buckwheat ground. Pa went to get man to shear sheep.

June, Saturday 14, 1879
Pleasant. Birt went to Corning. Real went with him as far as Ella's. Mr. Tom Souls shirred [sheared] sheep. Pat Smith exchanged cows with Pa. I went to Ella's after supes.

June, Sunday 15, 1879
Showery. Kit and Ella and I went to Sunday School to that school tour and to Woodtown. We ate dinner to Alice Barnard. Tid and Ella brought me home in the evening. Mrs. French went to girls.

June, Monday 16, 1879
Rained in the morning. Real washed and got some milkweed greens. Birt and Pa went to Corning and got a cow of big Fred. Ma sold her veal for $2.75. Planted some flowering beans.

June, Tuesday 17, 1879
Pleasant in the morning. Rained in the afternoon. We had some milk weed greens for dinner. Ella come up in the evening and Tid.

June, Wednesday 18, 1879
Pleasant. Charlie Finch come after some buckwheat. I cut my finger.

June, Thursday 19, 1879
Pleasant. Aurelia went to Frank's. Frank and Oscar brought her home. Frank took some cans to paint.

June, Friday 20, 1879
Pleasant. I helped Aunt Jane. Ella come up this afternoon a-foot. Tid came after her. Real's cow had a calf.

June, Saturday 21, 1879
Pleasant. I went to Flora's after supper. Tid come after.

June, Sunday 22, 1879
TIM'S Birthday [cousin]. Rained. I went to Sunday School – Ettie and I. We stayed down to Ella's till after four. We walked home. Alice and Emma and Mrs. Hunt was to Sunday School.

June, Monday 23, 1879
Pleasant. Birt and Pa commenced fixing the wagonhouse. Grandpa came over. Real and Ma washed. We fixed Frank's plants.

June, Tuesday 24, 1879
Pleasant. Pa went to Corning after lime in the afternoon. Birt and Pa drew stones for the barn. Ma ironed. I picked a hen. We had a pot pie for dinner. Real sewed. Ma had the headache.

June, Wednesday 25, 1879
Cloudy. Ma and Real went up to Aunt Delila's [Delila Wilts of Corning, age 60]. Went up to Flora's a few minutes. Pa went to Kitt Lewis after a jackscrew. Pa saw Manard Wolcott. Belle Weldon eloped.

June, Thursday 26, 1879
Rained a little in the evening. Pa went after Tom Straubinger to make some wall under the barn. WHITE clouds. My head aches.

June, Friday 27, 1879
Pleasant. Ma was sick all day. Tom commenced the wall.

June, Saturday 28, 1879
Rained. I went down home with Tom. Got wet. Mopped. The bees swarmed. I stayed all night with Aurelia.

June, Sunday 29, 1879
Rained. I stayed all night with Aurelia. They had chicken for dinner. Wanted to come home. Ella and Tid, Frank and Oscar and the children were here.

June, Monday 30, 1879
Pleasant. I stayed to Aurelia's. Aurelia come up to have Pa come after me. Tid had the horse. I have the backache.

July, Tuesday 1, 1879
Pleasant. Pa come after me. Aunt Jane came over after her cans. Aurelia gave me some calicos. Pa stopped to Aunt Delila's. Birt commenced haying.

July, Wednesday 2, 1879
Pleasant. Real picked strawberries up to Aunt Delila's. Pa went to mill. Aunt Jane gave me 10 shillings. Pa went to Grandpa's.

July, Thursday 3, 1879
Rained in the morning. Ma and Real went to Orley Gorton's. Birt dragged the buck wheat ground. Pa burnt some heaps. We had some greens for dinner.

July, Friday 4, 1879
Sprinkled a little. I stayed to home. Pa went to Corning and took Grandpa. He got me some firecrackers. The bees swarmed.

July, Saturday 5, 1879
Pleasant. Real and I picked peas. I killed a hen. Tid and Ella came up. Birt sowed buckwheat. I went to see if I could find some strawberries.

July, Sunday 6, 1879
Pleasant. I went to Sunday School - I and Ettie. Tid and Ella and Mrs. Cowen come up in the evening. Ma and Real went to Mrs. Marcy's. Pa went to Grandpas. Oscar stopped here.

July, Monday 7, 1879
Rained a little. Real and Ma washed. Real and I picked peas. Ella and Tid & Kitt & Mrs. Cowen & Miss French & Augusta Norton went to Watkins Glen.

June, Sunday 15. 1879.

I bow [?] met Ella and I went to Sunday School to [?] school house and to Wood town We ate dinner to Alpheus B [?] Lis and Ella brought me home in the evening My [?] [?] to give her

Monday 16.

rained in the morning pa washed out our some [?] no green. Lis and Sa went to [?] and got a cow of big Frush. Sa sould her veal for $2.15 planted some flowering Beans

Tuesday 17.

Pleasant in the morning rained in the aft We had some [?] need came for dinner Ella come up in the evening and [?]

June, Wednesday 18. 1879.

Pleasant Aurelia went to Franks Frank and Mary brought her home Frank took some cans to paint

Wednesday 18

Thursday 19.

Pleasant Charlie Finch come after some buck Wheat I cut my finger We had a frames[?]

Friday 20.

Pleasant I helped out pare Ella come up this afternoon a foot Tid came after her aunt Cow had a calf

July, Tuesday 8, 1879
Pleasant. Tid come up and fetched Rocket bare back. Real gave Tid some flour. Thristy Marcy come up and fetched Ellsey's baby. I went down to Thristy's.

July, Wednesday 9, 1879
Pleasant. Ma and Pa went to Corning. Ettie Howe come up. Real fixed the plants. Ma got her sows.

July, Thursday 10, 1879
Sprinkled a little. I wore my walking shoes for the first. Birt and Pa drawed hay.

July, Friday 11, 1879
We had a thundershower. Rained. Osly Gorton come here after some flour. Mrs. Wils stopped here till after the shower. Pa and Birt mowed the hay around the house.

July, Saturday 12, 1879
Pleasant. Frank come down. Oscar went to Corning. Real and I picked peas. I went to Frank's. Pa went to Caton Center.

July, Sunday 13, 1879
We had a shower. I went to Alice Thurber's with Oscar's folks. Went to meeting. Fred Brown brought me home. He come back to Oscar's.

July, Monday 14, 1879
Pleasant. Ma washed and Real. Birt mowed hay above Gorton's house. I picked peas.

July, Tuesday 15, 1879
Pleasant. Ma and Real and I ironed. Birt and Pa drawed hay.

July, Wednesday 16, 1879
Rained and the wind blew an apple tree out by the roots and blew the roof off from Ernest's house. Broke off some of the house plants. Laid Mr. Howe's fence flat. It took Birt's hat off. WHITE clouds.

July, Thursday 17, 1879
Pleasant. Real and I cut off our hair in front. We picked some red berries for a short cake. Grandpa ate dinner here. Birt mowed hay and Pa.

July, Friday 18, 1879
Pleasant. Frank and Oscar and there children come down. Oscar got some cider. Birt and Pa drawed hay.

July, Saturday 19, 1879
Pleasant. Ella and Tid come up this evening. I went home with them. Last night somebody's dog come and killed 21 sheep. For Pa they bit Old Bitty.

July, Sunday 20, 1879
Pleasant. I went to Sunday School. Jean and Julie come to French's. Ella and Tid brought me home.

July, Monday 21, 1879
Rained some. I went to Frank's - Pa and I. Real washed and ironed. I stopped to Delia's.

July, Tuesday 22, 1879
We had a hard Thundershower. Rained all night. Ella and Tid come up. Tid helped Pa. I picked some red raspberries. Canned the first fruit. Frank and Hattie Force came down and brought the hayfork. Real and Ella picked peas.

July, Wednesday 23, 1879
Cloudy. We painted the houseplants' dishes. Flora stopped. She was going to Ettie's. I picked some berries.

July, Thursday 24, 1879
Pleasant. Pa went to Corning. Tid come up in the afternoon and helped Pa. I had the headache in the forenoon. Real picked the sage. Ma washed her linen dress. I pealed apples to stew.

July, Friday 25, 1879
Pleasant. Oscar and Fred come down. I read some.

July, Saturday 26, 1879
Rained. I baked [a] cake. Real baked pies. Birt and Pa went to sleep. I rode the horses.

July, Sunday 27, 1879
Pleasant. I went to Sunday School I ate dinner to Kitt's. Kitt and I and Ella went to Frank's and to Sunday School on the hill. Ettie was there. Ritt and Ella stopped.

July, Monday 28, 1879
Pleasant. Real washed. I went to Oscar's.

July, Tuesday 29, 1879
Pleasant. I worked for Frank.

July, Wednesday 30, 1879
Pleasant.

July, Thursday 31, 1879
Pleasant. Frank and I went down to Fred's and Ist's.

August, Friday 1, 1879
Pleasant. Fred brought me home this morning. Tid and Ella come up. Pa and May went to mill. Ma went out [to] Hannah.

August, Saturday 2, 1879
Pleasant. I went down to Marcy's. Real and I picked some berries.

August, Sunday 3, 1879
Rained some. I went to Sunday School. Broke Ma's parisol. Kitt and Ella and I picked some blackberries. Tid and Ella brought me home.

August, Monday 4, 1879
Pleasant. We walked.

August, Tuesday 5, 1879
Pleasant. We ironed and I made [a] cake.

August, Wednesday 6, 1879
Pleasant. Mrs. Cowen and Ella come up. I and Ella went down to house. I went to Marcy's. Frank come after me this evening. I went home with her.

August, Thursday 7, 1879
Pleasant. Oscar went to Elmira. I and Fred went down to Charles' to play croquet.

August, Friday 8, 1879
Rained in the morning. Frank and Oscar went to the circus. I and Fred went to Mary's school. Mary stayed to Frank's to supper. We went to the circus. We had Ist's wagon.

August, Saturday 9, 1879
Cloudy. Frank and I gathered the peas. Fred and Mary and I went to Charlie's to play. Brought Mary – stayed all night with me.

August, Sunday 10, 1879
Pleasant. Fred and Mary went to Meeting. Mary and I went to Sunday School. Alice and I come to Oscar's. Fred and Mary brought me home.

August, Monday 11, 1879
Pleasant. Ma and Real washed.

August, Tuesday 12, 1879
Pleasant. Ella come up. Tid has got a horse and a cow. Mary Gorton come down to have Real help her fit a dress. Ma ironed. I went to Marcy's.

July, Monday 21. 1879.
Rained some
I went to Frank's & and I
real washed and ironed I stoped
to and delila's

Tuesday 22.
We had a hard Thunder Shower rained
all night. Ella and Tid came up
Tid helped Pa I picked some
red hay Lamie caried the first
fruit Frank and Hattie Force
came down brought the hay fork
Beal and Ellis picked peas

Wednesday 23.
Cloudy
We painted the house plants dishes
etc Flora stoped she was going to Ett...
I picked some berries

July, Thursday 24. 1879.
Plesant
Pa went to Corning Tid
came up in the afternoon and
helped Pa load the wagon
in the forenoon Beal picked
the sage Ma washed her engen
dress I pared apples to dry

Friday 25.
Plesant
Oscer and Fred come down
I red some

Saturday 26.
Rained
I backed cake Beal backed
pies Bert and Pa went to Ripley
I rode the horse

August, Wednesday 13, 1879
Sprinkled a little. I am 15 today. Ma got me a Bible stand & Real gave me a spread [bedspread?].

August, Thursday 14, 1879
Pleasant. Real went to Nealy's and Hattie Jones's. Pa went to the Center. Henry Beck come up to see Pa's heifer. I had Thristy, Ella, Hattie and Carrie and Miss Starner.

August, Friday 15, 1879
Cloudy. Ma mopped. I went to Marcy's. Pa went to Grandpa's. They had threshers. I packed a picknick. Birt finished plowing. I went a-riding. Went to Corning. I and Mary and Fred and Charlie.

August, Saturday 16, 1879
Rained. Real has got the headache. Pa and Birt went to Corning. Ma went to Ella's. Clem come up. Amelia and Carrie Seyter come up and stayed all night. Birt got Ma's parisol fixed.

August, Sunday 17, 1879
Rained a little. Amelia and Carrie and I went to Sunday School down to French's and up on the hill. Ella and Tid come up. Ella and Real went up to Oscar's. I rode down. The man came after Real's calf and Pa's heifer.

August, Monday 18, 1879
Cloudy. Ma washed. Birt, Pa and Real went to Corning. Kitt ✝ come up and stayed all night.

August, Tuesday 19, 1879
Pleasant. Kitt and I shot arrows. Kitt and I and Real went up to Oscar. Flora come a piece with us. Streavy come after Kitt.

August, Wednesday 20, 1879
Pleasant. Ma and Real and Ella went up to Frank's to help her. Pa went after Ell. Birt and Pa drew peas. I baked bread and I sewed. Fred brought the women home. He took me a-riding.

August, Thursday 21, 1879
Pleasant. Bill Williams died this morning at 7 o'clock. Birt went to Corning.

August, Friday 22, 1879
Pleasant. We went to Bill William's funeral. I had the headache.

August, Saturday 23, 1879
Pleasant. I went up to Flora's. Real mopped.

August, Sunday 24, 1879
Pleasant. Flora come down and took me to Sunday School in the afternoon. Flora and Ettie and I went to Sunday School up on the hill. Tid and Ella come up.

August, Monday 25, 1879
Rained a little. Ma and Real washed.

August, Tuesday 26, 1879
Pleasant. We cleaned the pantry. Thristy come up. Pa and Birt drawed manure.

August, Wednesday 27, 1879
Pleasant. We packed for the picknick. Kitt and Ella come up after flour. Mary Reasor come down and stayed all night. Fred stopped a while.

August, Thursday 28, 1879
PICKNICK. Pleasant. Ma and Birt & Real went to picknick. Mary and I and Miss Carvel and Charlie and Fred went to the picknick. Birt went to Corning.

August, Friday 29, 1879
Pleasant. Pa went to Corning. Mary Neal come and her sister. Real washed the windows. I washed my white dress.

August, Saturday 30, 1879
Pleasant. I ironed my white dress.

August, Sunday 31, 1879
Pleasant. I went to Sunday School. Ella and Tid brought me home. Thristy come up.

September, Monday 1, 1879
Pleasant. We washed. Mr. Howe's folks thrashed. Ma and Pa got me home.

September, Tuesday 2, 1879
Pleasant. I ironed by skirt and baked a cake. I went to Marcy's. Pa is 50 today.

September, Wednesday 3, 1879
Rained. I went to the picknick – had a nice time. I had an interduction to Edd Wolcott. Mary was there.

September, Thursday 4, 1879
Pleasant. Pa went to Corning. We had lima beans for supper. I went to Fred's. Stayed all night with Mary. We went to meeting. Mr. Ozmun preached.

September, Friday 5, 1879
Pleasant. I took breakfast to Fred. Forces visited Mary's school. I went to Frank's and stayed till after dinner. Oscar and Frank brought my home. Mary has written in my autograph [book].

September, Saturday 6, 1879
I went down to Marcy's. Thristy come up at night and brought my puffs. Ma had the headache. I mopped.

September, Sunday 7, 1879
Pleasant. Real's father [in-law] Seyter come up. Grandpa and Aunt Jane come over and stayed to dinner. Ettie come. Frank and the children drove down and brought Flora home. Ma and Real went up to Mrs. Gorton.

September, Monday 8, 1879
Cloudy. Real washed.

September, Tuesday 9, 1879
Showery. Ma and I has got bad colds. Ma ironed.

September, Wednesday 10, 1879
Pleasant. Pa went down to Ella's. She come up and stayed all day. The thrashers come. Tid helped thrash. Ella & Tid took Rocket and the red [wagon?] out west bound. Ella got her bed.

September, Thursday 11, 1879
Pleasant. The men here got threw thrashing. My headaches. Real got some corn. Our colds is better.

September, Friday 12, 1879
Cold and cloudy. My cold is better. Birt shot some pigeons. Flora come down. Bill Weldin and Thristy come up.

September, Saturday 13, 1879
Rained a little. Picnic day [at] the Gortons. Birt went to Corning.

September, Sunday 14, 1879
Pleasant. Frank and Oscar and the children come down. Frank brought me some bracelets. We had a pot pie for dinner. Walter N— [&] Mary Reasor stopped a minute. Mary's sisters and cousins.

September, Monday 15, 1879
Cloudy. We washed. Pa and Birt went to Corning. Ma and Real went up to the cornfield.

September, Tuesday 16, 1879
Rained some. Thundered. We dried some corn. Aunt Hannah and Uncle arrived and Mary Gregory come and stayed to dinner. Pa and Birt cleaned barley.

September, Wednesday 17, 1879
Pleasant. We cleaned the sitting room. Pa went to Elmira with barley. I went to Aunt Jane's after the carpet claw. Birt went to Corning. – Gorton helped Birt clean barley. The paper man came and a pedler.

AUGUST, WEDNESDAY 20. 1879.

Plesant
Ma and Beal and Ella went up to Frankes to help her Pa went after Ella Bert and Pa drawed pews I packed Bread and went Fred Daughter. ninen. home. he had me a riding

THURSDAY 21.

Plesant
Bill McComis died this morning at 7 oclock. Bert went to Corning

FRIDAY 22.

Plesant
We went to Billy McComis funeral I had the headache

AUGUST, SATURDAY 23. 1879.

Plesant
I went up to Floras Beal moped

SUNDAY 24.

Plesant
Flora come down and took me to Sunday School in the after noon Flora and Ettie and I went to Sunday School up on the hill Bert and Ella come up

MONDAY 25.

Rained a little
Ma and Beal washed I picked lue

September, Thursday 18, 1879
Cloudy. Ist come up. Pa and I gathered peaches. Grandpa ate dinner here.

September, Friday 19, 1879
Pleasant. Ma & Pa went to Corning. Ma got me some cloth for a dress skirt.

September, Saturday 20, 1879
Rained. Pa went to Elmira. Birt cut buckwheat. I went down to Ella. --- went with me. I sleep with Kitt.

September, Sunday 21, 1879
Pleasant. I and Kitt and Ella up to the garden. Ella and Tid brought me home.

September, Monday 22, 1879
Pleasant. Ma & Real washed. I went up to Oscar's tonight.

September, Tuesday 23, 1879
Pleasant. Oscar thrashed. I helped Frank.

September, Wednesday 24, 1879
Rained. Oscar brought me home. We canned peaches.

✝ **September, Thursday 25, 1879**
Pleasant. Ma and Real went to Sticklertown. Tid come up and got Ella's sheep. Pa & Birt commenced digging potatoes.

September, Friday 26, 1879
Pleasant. Pa went to Corning. Real blacked the stove. Ella and Kitt come up. Kitt and I went after chestnuts and grapes. Am —went with us.

September, Saturday 27, 1879
Pleasant. Ma has got the headache. Real and I filid [filled] 3 beds. Real and Birt went to Corning. Mrs. Gorton called.

September, Sunday 28, 1879
Pleasant. We put up the stove. I went down to Ist. Birt and I went up to Corning. Today is the last day of the Sunday School. Bob Seyter's folks is out.

September, Monday 29, 1879
Pleasant. I commenced drying apples. Ist [Therista Marcy] come up. Grandpa come over. Man and Real washed. Birt and Pa dug potatoes. Mr. Howe thrashed buckwheat.

September, Tuesday 30, 1879
Pleasant. Ma ironed and Real. Birt and Pa dug potatoes. Tid come up after me. I went down to sleep with Kitt.

October, Wednesday 1, 1879
Joacie Hufmann got Married. Pleasant. Kitt and I went a–riding. We went around the square. Pa went to Corning. Pa got some sausage.

October, Thursday 2, 1879
Pleasant. Ma went to Grandpa's. Aunt Nancy and Uncle Henry come and stayed all night.

October, Friday 3, 1879
Pleasant. Pa went to take Aunt Nancy home. Grandpa got a stove.

October, Saturday 4, 1879
Pleasant. Birt and Ma went to Elmira. Smoky.

October, Sunday 5, 1879
Pleasant. Ella and Bob and Charlie's folks come up.

October, Monday 6, 1879
Pleasant. Man and Real washed.

October, Tuesday 7, 1879
Pleasant. Real ironed. Ma had company. Mrs. Marcy and Mrs. Richards.

October, Wednesday 8, 1879
Pleasant. Pa went to the Center. Got my shoes fixed.

October, Thursday 9, 1879
Pleasant. Birt, Aurealia, Ma and I went to the fair.

October, Friday 10, 1879
Pa went to Corning. Flora rode up with Pa.

October, Saturday 11, 1879
Pleasant. Pa and Birt went to Corning took the butter. Henry come and stayed all night. Mr. Harrington is very low.

October, Sunday 12, 1879
Pleasant. Henry went home. Ella and Tid came up in the evening.

October, Monday 13, 1879
Pleasant. Real and Ma washed. I took up some plants.

October, Tuesday 14, 1879
Pleasant. I went to Grandpa's and got some dishes for plants. We had thrashers. Real ironed. Birt and Pa gathered apples.

October, Wednesday 15, 1879
Pleasant. Smoky. I helped Aunt Jane. Real commenced drying apples. Birt and Pa finished picking apples.

October, Thursday 16, 1879
Pleasant. I help Aunt Jane. Pa took the apples to the cider mill.

October, Friday 17, 1879
Rained. I help Aunt Jane. Mary Wolcott come up. Ella and Tid came. Birt set up with Mr. Harrington.

October, Saturday 18, 1879
Rained. Birt husked corn. Pa went to make cider and to learning.

October, Sunday 19, 1879
Rained in the morning. Sun shone in the afternoon. Pa and Ma went down to Ella's. Bob Cornish – Birt went home with him. Ist Marcy came. I went to Elsie's – took her some cider.

October, Monday 20, 1879
Pleasant. I worked for Aunt Jane. Pa and Birt helped Osley Gorton thrash. Birt set up with Mr. Harrington.

October, Tuesday 21, 1879
Pleasant. We ironed. Pa went to Corning. Fred come down and ask me to go to the dance Thursday night.

October, Wednesday 22, 1879
Pleasant. I went down to Mary's.

October, Thursday 23, 1879
Rained. I went to learning and to the dance. Ettie and I stayed all night.

October, Friday 24, 1879
Snowed. Oscar brought Ettie and I home this afternoon. I made the boas[?] for my dress.

October, Saturday 25, 1879
Pleasant. I mopped. Real and Ma cleaned the lamps. Real and I went to Grandpa's.

October, Sunday 26, 1879
Pleasant. Grandpa come over and got shaved. All of us went to Charlie Seyter's.

October, Monday 27, 1879
Pleasant. Real and Ma washed. Real and I gathered husks for a ✝ bed. Pa and Birt husked.

October, Tuesday 28, 1879
Rained. Pa went to Corning to mill. He took Osley's grist, too. Ma and Real ironed in the afternoon. Real and I gathered husks. Oscar come and borrowed the wagon.

October, Wednesday 29, 1879
Pleasant. I helped Aunt Jane.

October, Thursday 30, 1879
Pleasant. I helped Aunt Jane. Ella come up. Birt went to Corning with Oscar. He left Lea here and Ma helped him. Pa took Ella home.

October, Friday 31, 1879
Cold. Pa and Birt went to Sticklertown. Ma washed a bed tick. Real and I slitted husks.

November, Saturday 1, 1879
Snowed. I went to Ella's – stayed all night. Henry killed the white kitten.

November, Sunday 2, 1879
Pleasant and cloudy. Real and Birt come down to Ella's. I came home with them.

November, Monday 3, 1879
Snowed. Ma and Real washed. Birt and Tid went a-hunting. Pa and I and Ma cracked some hickory nuts. I commenced ripping up my dress.

November, Tuesday 4, 1879
Snowed. Election. Pa went to the Center. Birt went to Corning. Real cleaned the dining room. Ma had the headache. I went to Grandpa's.

November, Wednesday 5, 1879
Cloudy. Birt went to Sticklertown. I went to Grandpa's. We moved the plants.

November, Thursday 6, 1879
Cloudy. Real and Birt went to Oscar's. Pa went to the Center.

November, Friday 7, 1879
Pleasant. Pa and Birt killed the bull and went to Corning. Ma and I finished tearing up the husks and Real.

November, Saturday 8, 1879
Pleasant. Pa and Birt went to Corning. Real and I got the cows. I mopped.

November, Sunday 9, 1879
Cloudy. I and Pa went to Frank's a little while. I went up to Flora's. Rained in the evening.

November, Monday 10, 1879
Pleasant. Tom come up to work at the wall. Ma and Real washed. Pa went to Corning.

November, Tuesday 11, 1879
Rained. Real ironed.

November, Wednesday 12, 1879
Rained. Henry come up. Ma and Real washed the blankets.

November, Thursday 13, 1879
Pleasant. Tom Straubinger finished the wall and --- all. Charlie Seyter come. Pa paid Tom $4.37.

November, Friday 14, 1879
Rained. Real and I cleaned the Parlor. Henry Seyter come.

November, Saturday 15, 1879
Rained. Birt went to Corning – took Henry Seyter to Corning. Aunt Jane come over.

November, Sunday 16, 1879
Cloudy. We cleaned all day.

November, Monday 17, 1879
Cloudy. Real and Ma washed. I churned and ironed. Mary, Toby and Christopher come up. Pa and Birt went to Osley's.

November, Tuesday 18, 1879
Snowed. We ironed. Osley come down. I commenced gray dress.

November, Wednesday 19, 1879
Pleasant. We ciled [sealed] the logs. Ella and Tid come up in the evening.

November, Thursday 20, 1879
Snowed. Blowed. We made the sausage and tried the lard. Osley come down and he took a spare rib.

November, Friday 21, 1879
Pleasant. Aunt Delia come down and give me a present for my birthday — a tidy [any of various articles for keeping things tidy, as a box having small drawers and compartments]. Pa and Birt went to Corning and got a stove for Real. Real mopped. Pa has got the headache. I have got a cold bad.

November, Saturday 22, 1879
Pleasant. Real and Birt went to Corning and got those dishes and me some yarn. Pa boiled the hogs' heads. Ma made some brine. Pa sent his butter to Corning and they didn't take it.

November, Sunday 23, 1879
Pleasant. Ella and Tid come up. Will Marcy come and Ist. Will Hunt come. I went home with Ella. Will Marcy come home last night.

November, Monday 24, 1879
Pleasant. I went to school. TIM COME HERE. Run away. Gill come and got him.

November, Tuesday 25, 1879
Pleasant. I went to school.

October, Saturday 25. 1879.

Plesant
I mooped keal and the
cleand the lamps
Real and I went to Grand

Sunday 26.

Plesant
Grandpa come over and got
Shaved all of us went
to Charlie Seyors

Monday 27.

Plesant
Real and Ma worked
Real and I gathered
husks for a bed
Pa and Bert husks

October, Tuesday 28. 1879.

Rained
Pa went to Corning
to mill he took Orley's
grist to. Ma and Real
Iuned In the four room
Real and I gathered husks
Lucu come and borrowed the
iron.

Wednesday 29.

Plesant
I helped aunt Jane.

Thursday 30.

Plesant
I helped aunt Jane. Ella
come up. Bert went to Corning
with Orcer he left tea
hear and Ma shiped him
Pa took Ella home

November, Wednesday 26, 1879
Pleasant. I went to school. I come home a-foot. Clem was here. He come to bid us good bye. Birt went to the mill.

November, Thursday 27, 1879
THANKSGIVING. Pleasant. Pa and Birt went a-hunting. Birt and Real went to housekeeping.

November, Friday 28, 1879
Rained. I went to school. Flora and Delia and Irena was there. I brought John home. Real went up to Aunt Delia's. Birt plowed.

November, Saturday 29, 1879
Snowed. Ma washed. I mopped. Ma ironed.

November, Sunday 30, 1879
Pleasant. I and Ma and Pa ate dinner upstairs to Real and Birt's.

December, Monday 1, 1879
Pleasant. I went to school. Pa went to Corning. I had the headache.

December, Tuesday 2, 1879
Cloudy. I went to school.

December, Wednesday 3, 1879
Cloudy. I went to school. Ella went up to Mrs. Woodard. Oscar come down. He had his sister-in-law. He brought wood.

December, Thursday 4, 1879
Cloudy. I went to school.

December, Friday 5, 1879
Pleasant. I went to school. I went home. Had chicken pie.

December, Saturday 6, 1879
XXX. Rained. I mopped. Celia and Thurston and Laura canned some apples.

December, Sunday 7, 1879
Pleasant. I went up to Flora Bundy's - Ettie and I. Real and Birt come down. Pa went to meeting up on the hill.

December, Monday 8, 1879
Pleasant and snowed. Pa brought me to Ella's. I went to school. Ma washed. Real wisked. Birt went a-hunting. Pa went to Corning.

December, Tuesday 9, 1879
Cloudy. I went to school. Ella had the headache.

December, Wednesday 10, 1879
Rained. I went to school. I have got a bad cold.

December, Thursday 11, 1879
Rained. I went to school. Ella and Tid went up home and to Oscar's.

December, Friday 12, 1879
Pleasant. I went to school. I went home.

December, Saturday 13, 1879
Cold. I mopped and churned. Aunt Delia come down and brought me a doll to dress and Real a pale of soot [probably to be used for gardening]. Pa went to Corning.

December, Sunday 14, 1879
Pleasant. I stayed to home. Pa went to Grandpa's.

December, Monday 15, 1879
Snowed. Ma finished my dress. Pa brought me down to Ella's. Birt went to the Center.

December, Tuesday 16, 1879
Pleasant. I went to school I had the headache.

December, Wednesday 17, 1879
Snowed. I went to school.

December, Thursday 18, 1879
Pleasant. I went to school. Ella went up to Gersh's.

December, Friday 19, 1879
Pleasant. I went home. I went to school.

December, Saturday 20, 1879
Cloudy. I went up to Aunt Delia's. She gave me some Medleys. I also mopped. Ettie went up to Miss Harrington's.

December, Sunday 21, 1879
Pleasant. Ella and tid come up. I went up with them. Ma had a pain in her side.

December, Monday 22, 1879
Pleasant. I went to school. Ella sewed. Hattie Wilcox commenced school.

December, Tuesday 23, 1879
Pleasant. I went to school. George Hunt come a-visiting. Birt come down and helped Tid kill a bull.

December, Wednesday 24, 1879
Cloudy. I went to home.

December, Thursday 25, 1879
Snowed. Frank stopped. I stayed to home.

December, Friday 26, 1879
Pleasant. Ettie came here after Real's mannequin.

December, Saturday 27, 1879
Pleasant. I mopped and packed. Ettie brought back Real's mannequin.

December, Sunday 28, 1879
I had company – Carrie. Charlie Seyter's folks and Ella and Tid. Ella and I went home with them.

December, Monday 29, 1879
Cloudy. I went to school. Ma and Real went to Corning.

December, Tuesday 30, 1879
Snowed. I went to school. Ma washed.

December, Wednesday 31, 1879
Hailed. I went to school and come home and met Pa coming after me.

January, Thursday 1, 1880
Pleasant. I got a pair of stockings. We all went up to Osley's on a bobsled.

January, Friday 2, 1880
Pleasant. I went to school [and to] Flora's house.

January, Saturday 3, 1880
Rained. I and Ma went to Frank Howe's. Paid his tax.

[She skipped some days]

January, Sunday 18, 1880
Ettie and Anna Robinson come here. Mary Reasor was married.

January, Sunday 23, 1889
We went to Nealy Niver's funeral. She died Friday night. I went to Kitt's party Sunday and Nancy's to stay.

February, Sunday 1, 1880
I went to Ella's with Pa. Pa went after Ma down to Marcy's.

February, Monday 4, 1880 [Monday is not correct]
Ma and Real went down to Ella's with Pa. He went to Corning.

February, Sunday 8, 1880
Birt's pa died.

December, Wednesday 24. 1879.

Cloudy
I went I went
home

Thursday 25.

Snowed
Spook stop
I stade to home

Friday 26.

Plesant
Ettie came hear after
Reals lamerquin

December, Saturday 27. 1879.

Plesant
I moped and picked
Ettie braught
back Reals lambrequin

Sunday 28.

Plesant
I had Company Carrie
Marlier Sigler folks
and Elza and Lod Ettie
I went home with them

Monday 29.

Cloudy
I went to School
Maud Rea went
to corning

February, Sunday 15, 1880
I saw thunderheads. Ella, Tid, Kitt came here. Ettie went to Flora's. School was out. Frida.

February, Sunday 22, 1880
Ella and Tid come after dinner. Bob and Mrs. Richardson come to Birt's. Tid had the toothache.

February, Sunday 29, 1880
Birt, Pa and I went to Tom's and brought Amelia home with us. She stayed till Monday.

March, Sunday 7, 1880
I have got a sore throat. Birt and Pa went to Mr. Harrington's.

End of Diary

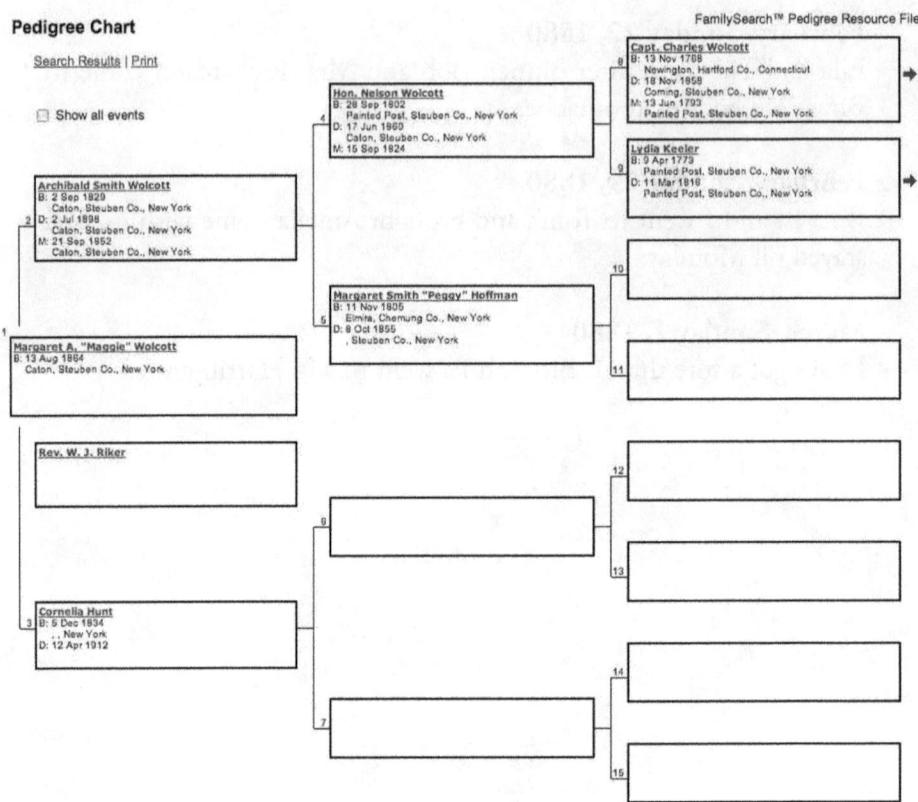

Maggie's pedigree chart from FamilySearch.org

Afterward

Maggie married J. Willett [sometimes Willet or Willett J.] Riker on December 21, 1887. Willett was a minister in several locations. Between 1891-1892 they lived in Auburn, New York. In 1893 they lived in Alton, New York. In 1900 the census listed her and Willett living in Binghamton on Cherry Street. Willett was the minister of First Free Methodist Church of Binghamton. Between 1900-1903 Willett was the minister for the Rose Free Methodist Church in Rose, New York. In 1904 they lived in Fulton, New York. They eventually had two children Mary [Simcoe] and Cornelia [Park]. In the 1910 census they lived in Corning, New York on South Elm Street. In the 1920 census Willet worked at Corning Glass. J. Willett lived in South Corning but died at his daughter's home in Apalachin in 1927. Our research team has not yet found when Maggie died [still alive 1933 on Elm Street, sick 1935 not in directory 1936] or where she is buried.

The Wolcott family traces back to England to Galdon House in Somerset to Henry Wolcott circa 1558. The family came to America in May 1630 and landed in Dorcester, Massachusetts.

- Diane Janowski

Bibliography

Lawyer, William S. *Binghamton: Its Settlement, Growth and Development and the Factors in its History.* Century Memorial Publishing Company, 1900

Dennis, Frank. "Ministers, Town of Rose, Wayne County, NY." . 14 December 2000. . 28 December2100 <http://webcache.googleusercontent.com/search?q=cache:AHdXq_Cl-5cJ:wayne.nygenweb.net/rose/rosemins.html+%22willet+riker%22&cd=3&hl=en&ct=clnk&gl=us&client=safari>.

New York Atlas. Caton, Caton Center, New York: D.G. Beers & Co., 1873.

More diaries from
New York State teenagers of the 1800s

Queen City Adventure
Home in these Hills
A Darned Good Time
A Year in the Life of a Country Girl
My Centennial Diary
Plank Road Explorer
Ontario Breeze

Visit our website or your favorite bookstore

www.NewYorkHistoryReview.com

www.ingramcontent.com/pod-product-compliance
Lightning Source LLC
Chambersburg PA
CBHW031656040426
42453CB00006B/326